trotman

Real
Life

GUIDES

RETAIL

Dee Pilgrim

2nd edition

Real Life Guides: Retail
This 2nd edition published in 2008 by Trotman,
an imprint of Crimson Publishing Ltd, Westminster House,
Kew Road, Richmond, Surrey, TW9 2ND.

First edition published in 2004 by
Trotman and Company Ltd

© Trotman 2004, 2007

Author Dee Pilgrim
Advertising Sarah Talbot, Advertising Sales Director

Design by XAB

British Library Cataloguing in Publications Data
A catalogue record for this book is available
from the British Library

ISBN 978 1 84455 154 5

Typeset by Ellipsis Books Ltd, Glasgow
Printed and bound in Great Britain by
MPG Books Ltd, Bodmin

Real
Life

GUIDES

CONTENTS

About the author

Dee Pilgrim studied journalism at the London College of Printing before working on a variety of music and women's titles. As a freelancer and a full-time member of staff she has written numerous articles and interviews for *Company, Cosmopolitan, New Woman, Woman's Journal* and *Weight Watchers* magazines. As a freelancer for Independent Magazines she concentrated on celebrity interviews and film, theatre and restaurant reviews for such titles as *Ms London, Girl About Town, LAM* and *Nine to Five* magazines, and in her capacity as a critic she has appeared on both radio and television. When not attending film screenings she is active within the Critics' Circle, co-writes songs and is currently engaged in writing the narrative to an as yet unpublished trilogy of children's illustrated books.

Acknowledgements

Thank you to all the people who so kindly agreed to be interviewed for this book including Claudia Mihalache, Howies Clothing, Jonathan Baron and Sarah Welsh.

For her detailed analysis and comments on the retail industry many thanks to Anne Richardson, Careers Strategy Manager, Skillsmart Retail and also to Beverley Paddey, Head of Standards & Qualifications of Skillsmart Retail for her help on the training chapter.

Foreword

Nobody can say that the retail industry is uniform. From the local corner shop to the large multi-national chains, no two businesses have identical needs, markets or challenges. However each retailer is only as good as the staff that run the business on a day-to-day basis. Those that can keep their staff prepared and motivated to face the challenges of this most competitive of industries will prosper; those who can't, won't.

City & Guilds are delighted to be part of the Trotman *Real Life Guides* series to help raise your awareness of these vocational qualifications. Our qualifications in retail have been designed with this diversity in mind. Each contains a wide range of units to allow learners and employers to tailor them to their requirements. See www.cityandguilds.com for more details.

The Retail Team
City & Guilds

Introduction

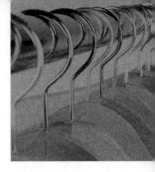

It's become something of a joke to talk about people who 'shop until they drop', but the retail business is anything but a joke. In fact, retailing – the process of selling goods to customers and all that this entails – is a very serious business that we all interact with every day of our lives. Just think about it for a moment: the clothes you are wearing have all been designed, manufactured and then bought from a retail outlet such as a boutique or department store; the food you eat came from a shop, most probably a supermarket; even this book you are reading could well have come from a W H Smith or a Waterstones. You will have local shops near to where you live, maybe a large supermarket in the area, and the high street of any town or city will be a bustling place with people intent on buying everything from TVs to bedding, while others will be just as keen to sell to them.

Over the last five years employment in retailing has grown by over 86,700 and with the UK economy still growing at a slow but steady rate the retail sector is bound to continue to expand.

Just how all-encompassing the world of retail is becomes clear when you read the figures. In 2006 the total figure for UK retail sales was approximately £256 billion – that's larger than the combined economies of both Denmark and

Portugal. There are now approximately 278,365 retail outlets operating in the UK. According to the Office of National Statistics, in 2006 the retail industry employed over 2.9 million people. That is a staggering 11 per cent of the total UK workforce, meaning one in every nine working people is in retail. Over the last five years employment in retailing has grown by over 86,700 and with the UK economy still growing at a slow but steady rate the retail sector is bound to continue to expand. In fact, vacancies for graduates have increased in retailing in the last few years while they have largely declined in other industries. However, you don't have to have a degree to get into this business as many companies offer training on the job and some have training schemes that even lead to National Vocational Qualifications (NVQs).

Once upon a time a job in retail was not seen as either particularly exciting or sexy but that's certainly not the case now. With everybody wanting to buy, buy, buy, the opportunities to sell, sell, sell have broadened out massively. The growth of retail parks, American-style shopping malls and the huge increase in the mail order and internet (e-tailing) markets means we can buy more things in more ways than ever before and so jobs within the retail trade are changing in order to reflect these trends. In fact, things change on the High Street (the industry's term for the major retail shops) so quickly you have to be a smart operator not to miss the boat. In recent years sales for such well-known names as Marks & Spencer, W H Smith and Sainsbury's have all suffered because they failed to spot customer trends, especially the burgeoning youth market. These major retailers all had to make changes, and quickly, to turn their fortunes around.

Aggressive TV advertising campaigns for Marks & Spencer (fashion shoots including supermodels Twiggy and Erin O'Connor, and 'this is not just any food, this is Marks & Spencer food') proved to be massively successful, while Sainsbury's cut prices and introduced more organic foods and new ranges such as 'Taste the Difference' in order to woo back customers. This is why retailing is an exciting business to be in, it moves fast, it constantly changes and it challenges its employees to keep coming up with new ways to part consumers from their money.

We may only see the people on the shop floor but there are plenty of 'hidden' jobs in retailing. As consumers we may only interact with the cashiers or sales assistants but there are also buyers, managers, marketing teams and distributors who all ensure we get the products we want to buy at the right time and at the right price.

In fact, jobs in retailing are split into nine main areas.

- Buying

- Finance

- Human resources

- Information technology (IT)

- Logistics

- Marketing and public relations (PR)

DID YOU KNOW?

By 2008, the UK's DIY and hardware market is estimated to be worth in the region of £16.1 billion with the leading products being paint, wall-lining and wallpaper (21.6 per cent of the total market value).

- Merchandising
- Store operations (90 per cent of all jobs fall into store ops)
- Visual merchandising.

For the purposes of this book we shall be concentrating on those closest to the core of the retail trade, those involved with the actual buying and selling, although related businesses are mentioned so you can make a more informed choice as to which area within the industry you would like to work.

It's also good to remember that retail is a relatively youthful industry, with 29 per cent of all employees between 16 and 24 years old. Many young people enter at the bottom of the career ladder but quickly progress to the top. Some even get to be board members by the time they are 40 – still others go on to own the whole company!

If you are considering a job in retailing then this book will help you to make up your mind. Not only will it explain what positions are actually available, but it will also describe what different people actually do within the industry. It will tell you what qualities and skills you will need to get on and what personality traits will hold you back. It will explain how you can train and where you can look to find that all-important first job. Finally, the case studies will demonstrate just how varied jobs within the industry can be. A future career in retailing isn't a hard sell because this is an industry with great things ahead of it, and just think, you could be a part of it.

KEY TERMS

Like most industries retailing has its own set of terms used for specific situations. Here is a list of the most commonly used retail jargon.

Business to Business (B2B)

This means when one business sells to another.

Business to Consumer (B2C)

This is what happens when you go into a shop and buy something.

Bricks and Mortar Businesses

Traditional businesses that actually have shops and salesrooms rather than carrying out their business electronically.

Chip and Pin

New technology is extremely important in the retail trade with innovative systems constantly coming through to streamline transactions between staff and customers. The new Chip and Pin system, whereby you are assigned a four-digit PIN (personal identification number) for your debit or credit card has significantly cut the amount of time it takes to pay for items at tills. Customers no longer have to sign a paper receipt when they pay for goods, they simply insert their card into a special reader, and then key in their PIN. This is proving to be a much more secure method of payment because only the person the card is assigned to should ever know their PIN.

DID YOU KNOW?

In 2006 people in Britain spent £1.9 billion on organic food, drink and textiles — 22 per cent more than in 2005. However, this is still less than 1.6 per cent of all UK food sales.

Clicks and Mortar Businesses
A business that sells its goods through a combination of traditional outlets and electronically (see below).

E-commerce/E-tailing
These are sales carried out electronically over the Internet as opposed to bricks and mortar sales.

C-shops
Once known as the humble corner shop, or local convenience store, this is now one of the biggest growth areas in retail. Both Tesco and Sainsbury's have tried to muscle in on this market with Tesco Metro and Sainsbury's Local stores, with the other big supermarket groups queuing up to buy job lots of c-shops. However, the big names are still Spar, Co-op and Londis.

The High Street
Where once this term applied literally to the shops on your local high street it now applies to all the well-known larger retail chains that have a presence in our towns and cities including Sainsbury's, Tesco, Marks & Spencer, Next, Dixons and W H Smith.

Point of Sale (POS)
This refers to the physical location at which goods are sold to customers, often a promotional display unit.

T-commerce
Sales carried out through the television.

HOWIES CLOTHING

Success story

Running a clothing firm was never the first choice of career for husband and wife team David and Clare Hieatt, the couple behind the Howies ethical clothing range (the name comes from Clare's maiden name of Howells).

In the mid 1990s they were both very busy working in high-powered jobs in advertising and design in London, but wanted to find a range of clothing that would fit in with their very active, outdoor pursuits lifestyle of canoeing and mountain biking. They also wanted it to be eco-friendly. Unfortunately, there was nothing on the High Street that fitted their particular criteria and so, in 1995, they decided to start their own brand.

From the start Howies was different from traditional forms of clothing retail because it was (and in the main still is) an e-commerce venture. David and Clare were very clear about the kind of individuals who would buy their brand

At Howies we have developed a very strong brand because we have set out to build something we believe in.

– the extreme sports fans who were into BMX bikes, skateboarding and canoeing just like them – so they tailored their website and their designs to appeal specifically to those individuals. They began with four boxes of organic cotton T-shirts on their living-room floor with family and friends roped in to help with the initial financing, the marketing, designing and selling.

With no background in fashion retail David and Clare had to trust their instincts they were on to the right thing. Their passion and commitment to environmental issues, and their production of T-shirts and jeans that were hard wearing and long lasting, soon paid off as their quirky designs (one of their T-shirts doubles as an organ donor card) proved very popular with the skateboarding and BMX biking communities around Britain. Before long they were selling their designs via a number of clothing boutiques, at extreme sports shows and rallies, and their catalogue had become a labour of love with as much space dedicated to explaining about the environmental impact of the Howies brand as actually selling the clothes.

After six years of hard slog and constant stress over cash flow, David and Clare decided to move the company to the small Welsh costal town of Cardigan in 2001. Then came their biggest battle when clothing giant Levi Strauss took offence at Howies' using name tabs on its jeans. Levi Strauss wanted the tabs removed because it said the red name tab on Levi's jeans was one of its USPs (unique selling points). The couple used all their PR and marketing skills to get this David and Goliath fight into the press, and sensing this was one battle where it would not win the hearts and minds of consumers, Levi Strauss backed down.

In 2005 Howies secured a £550,000 grant from Finance Wales (a branch of the Welsh Development Agency) and with this money was able to expand its clothing range and to source alternative, eco-friendly materials. It also employed a production technologist to find new ways of producing clothing as naturally as possible. In the same year, with the Howies brand now sold worldwide (you can buy Howies T-shirts and jeans in Paul Smith boutiques in Japan), sales doubled to almost £6 million. 'Our external company image is different and crazy, but we are very well run on the inside,' says David Hieatt. 'This has helped us succeed, along with our clear vision of where we are going.'

However, the Hieatts still felt they needed more money to expand further and having thoroughly researched the only three companies around that seemed to share their core values, they finally sold Howies to the US company Timberland in 2006 for an undisclosed sum. In Autumn 2007 a Howies retail shop opened on Carnaby Street in London. David and Clare will continue to oversee the company's day-to-day running. On the Howies website David explains that doing business with Timberland just felt right. 'At Howies we have developed a very strong brand because we have set out to build something we believe in,' he says. 'The deal with Timberland will allow us to grow further while maintaining all our standards and values.'

To find out more about Howies visit the website at www.howies.co.uk.

PETER DODD

Case study 1

THE BUYER

*When 35-year-old Peter left school at 16
he went straight into the retail business,
working on the shopfloor for sportswear
company Cobra Sports.*

His training was very hands on, dealing
with customers, getting involved with
deliveries and stock, and liaising with the
management and head office. He quickly
worked his way through the company,
moving from sales associate (assistant) to
assistant manager, then manager and area
manager when he became involved with
trouble-shooting (including the hiring and
firing of staff) for the firm's West End store.
After ten years he felt there was nowhere
left for him to go so he moved sideways to
the company's warehouse in Chiswick. This
dealt with all the Cobra Sports stores in
London and Peter was responsible for the
logistical side of things, sorting out POS
stock, the inventory and handling an awful
lot of deliveries. After three years, Peter
was made redundant just before the firm
went bankrupt. He then worked for Talbots

You really
have to
have a
logical,
no-nonsense,
let's get
the job
done,
hands-on
attitude to
do what
I do.

ladies' fashion retailer and Soletrader shoe stores before joining DKNY.

Mainly working out of the Donna Karan DKNY store in London's Bond Street Peter is now a buyer/stock controller for the company.

'I basically just got fed up with the shop floor side of retail – always having to work at weekends and on late-night shopping evenings. That really got me down and also, if I'm honest, I had lost interest in selling, it didn't offer me a challenge any more. Now I am really involved with the buying side for DKNY. I liaise with New York (where the company originated) every day mainly by telephone or fax and that means getting into the office as early as 7am or 8am because of the time difference and I like to iron out any problems before the shop in Bond Street, actually opens. I am part of a team of buyers and my responsibility is buying the fabrics we use to make our clothes.

'There's a company called Premier Vision in France and they bring over new fabrics twice a year and I frequently visit them as well. I also visit our warehouse in Holland where I oversee the quality control. I go and see the people, organise what we are buying and what costings we have budget-wise and once the material comes to us here I then organise its redistribution to

Portugal and to the Philippines where our garments are made. I also have to liaise with the management team and our visual team and work out what is selling where, so if something is selling well in Cheshire and not in London I will organise the redistribution of the surplus stock. I also organise promotions, like we had a PURE event to promote our cotton and pure linen ranges and I organised the production of freshly prepared smoothies in our in-store bar.

'You really have to have a logical, no-nonsense, let's get the job done, hands-on attitude to do what I do. The things I like most about working here are the regular Monday to Friday hours, the fact the money is very good and the team is great. I also get to travel for my job – apart from France and Holland I have also visited New York once or twice. However, I see this (my job) as a bit of a stepping-stone and I really want to progress here at DKNY in the next four or five years. There is the possibility of being relocated State-side or of becoming overall logistics co-ordinator for the company. I would also really like to achieve more recognition within the company. To go out on a high would be to source and to buy in a fabric that becomes the talk of the season. Something like the new Prince of Wales check!'

What's the story?

Long gone are the days when we were all fiercely loyal to particular brands and specific shops – shopping in Sainsbury's because that's where our mums went, or always buying Levi's because that's what everyone else bought. Nowadays, shoppers have much more choice and are much more savvy, looking for the best bargains, keeping up with the newest trends by surfing the internet, even shopping ethically by sourcing Fairtrade or organic products. Because shoppers have sharpened up their act, the retailers have been forced to buck their own ideas up and must now constantly adapt to the desires and needs of their customers.

At present, the retail market is split into the following main categories:

- Chainstore
- Clothing and footwear

- DIY/hardware
- Electrical appliances
- Food/groceries
- Furniture
- Leisure/entertainment
- Luxury
- Small store
- Supermarket.

Some of these categories are set to grow at a faster pace than others, as Anne Richardson, Careers Strategy Manager at Skillsmart Retail, the Sector Skills Council for the retail trade, points out. 'The luxury goods market is still growing in line with the cult of celebrity. They go hand in hand as people want to wear a label because they've seen Posh Spice wearing it,' she says. 'Predictably, IT and gadgets are still going strongly – like everyone wanting to get their hands on the new iPhone, and specialist food and kitchen shops such as Cucina and Divertimenti are doing surprisingly well on the back of TV food shows by names such as Nigella Lawson, Rick Stein and Jamie Oliver.'

However, the area where growth is set to go through the roof is not in one of the specific categories listed above, but in the way we buy our goods. 'Online is growing phenomenally,' says Richardson. 'At present it is only 4 per cent of all sales, but the prediction is it will rise to 25 per cent in the next ten years. The reason for this is people are more confident of ordering online these days. Also, older people are becoming more adept at using the internet – the silver surfers – and they find ordering via the net and getting goods delivered to their homes a very convenient way to shop.'

But the growth of the internet does not mean retail stores are set to vanish, indeed as Richardson explains, in the next few years we are going to see tremendous growth in the amount of new retail outlets opening. This means there will be even more jobs available within the sector. 'We estimate between 300,000 and half a million new jobs will be created in the retail sector over the next three to five years. This is due to major new developments that are currently in the process of being built,' she explains. 'These include White City (where the BBC has its media hub), which is being developed because of the Olympics, the Eagle Centre in Derby (where 4,000 new jobs will become available), the Broadmarsh Centre in Nottingham (8,000 new jobs), and St David's 2 in Cardiff (at least 5,000 new jobs). On top of this every year at least 1.2 million jobs in retail need filling due to "churn" (people retiring, moving out of the retail area, moving on to upper management, or taking career or maternity breaks). There is also a high turnover because many people stay in the sector for less than a year, while some stay only three months.'

This high turnover is due to a number of factors, the most important being low expectations of the job.

Traditionally, people working in retail were not seen as being particularly well qualified or talented, although this perception has changed since new industry-wide qualifications have been put into place. The other problem has been potential candidates have ignored the sector because they have not been aware of the diversity of jobs on offer. In 2004, a Careers Strategy Group was formed and the Retail Careers Strategy was developed to:

● Improve the promotion of careers in retail to young people

● Enhance the status and credibility of jobs and careers in retail

● Change the perception of key influencers – parents and careers advisers

● Raise awareness among retailers of the influence they can have and how working together can help to promote retail careers.

'A lot of people who do degrees don't realise the amount of different areas and roles in retail,' says Richardson. 'In fact, some of them start doing a business and finance course with no interest in retail at all, and yet a lot of big money is to be made in the business and finance areas of retail. Marketing is another area where people do not build a direct correlation between the shop floor and the end product, yet the marketing sector in retail is massive.'

> **DID YOU KNOW?**
>
> John Lewis re-launched its website in 2007 so that a further 19,000 products could be added to its existing online range of 22,000 items. The move was due to demand after sales rose from 2006's level by 44 per cent.

All of this is good news if you feel a career in retail could be for you because the opportunities are definitely out there. In fact, the UK's top retailers are all vying with each other for the best candidates, especially in the less visible areas you might not immediately associate with buying and selling. Along with the jobs in finance and marketing mentioned above these also include many roles in middle management, and specialist areas such as food technologists and garment technologists.

You may also like to consider two areas that are not as immediately obvious as the shops on the High Street. These are wholesaling and import/export.

According to United Nations legislation, the definition of wholesaling is 'the resale (sale without transformation) of new and used goods to retailers, to industrial, commercial, institutional or professional users, or to other wholesalers . . . Wholesalers frequently physically assemble, sort and grade goods in large lots, break bulk, repack and redistribute in smaller lots.' What this basically means is wholesalers buy goods in bulk, repackage the goods into smaller units, which they then sell on to other retailers.

Import/export is when a company or individual buys goods from one country – say jeans from Thailand or China – and imports them into another, such as this country. They may then export them on to other regions such as Canada or America. Importers/exporters need to have really good financial brains as different countries tend to have varying import/export taxes and duties (dependent on trade agreements) and so working out if it is financially viable to import certain goods is essential to cash flow.

Now you know more about the overall retail area it's time to look at what jobs you can actually do within it. It doesn't matter if you have fairly modest ambitions or if you want to end up running the whole company, the job base is so wide you are bound to find something that suits you and your particular skills.

What are the jobs?

4

DID YOU KNOW?

B&Q stores are being given a multimillion-pound makeover in a bid to attract more women. The aim is to make the stores feel 'softer' and less like builder's merchants. The new look has been launched with a TV ad campaign featuring B&Q's new strapline 'Let's Do It' shown during the breaks in Coronation Street.

While many of us view buying things and even window shopping as a pretty fun thing to do, most of us would probably not have considered that a job selling can also be great fun and very rewarding. The world of retail never stands still and new technology means retailers are often the first to employ electronic tools such as scanners and computerised tills. But there is far more to retailing than just buying and selling and in this chapter we will explore just what it is different people within the retailing world actually do. As stated previously, this book deals mainly with the people closest to the core of retailing which includes those who work on the shop floor and also the managers, buyers, and display staff who work in and around the stores and also at head office. We will also be looking at associated careers such as marketing and distribution. The chart below gives you some idea of the variety of jobs you can do in the retail trade.

JOBS IN RETAIL

In the warehouse
DISTRIBUTORS
LOGISTICS CO-ORDINATOR
TRANSPORT STAFF

In the store
ASSISTANT MANAGER
CHECKOUT STAFF
CUSTOMER SERVICE STAFF (CUSTOMER SERVICE DESK)
DEPARTMENT SALES MANAGER
PERSONAL SHOPPER
PRODUCE ASSISTANT
RECEIVING SUPERVISOR (STOCKROOM STAFF)
SALES ASSISTANT
VISUAL DISPLAY ASSISTANT

At head office
BUYER
HUMAN RESOURCES
IT/TECHNICAL BACK UP
MARKETING
MERCHANDISING
PR DEPARTMENT

In other locations
CALL CENTRE STAFF
DESIGNERS
FOOD TECHNOLOGISTS
GARMENT TECHNOLOGISTS
MANUFACTURERS/PRODUCERS

Before looking at these jobs in greater detail, let's first explore what your work environment will be like – just where is it you will actually be working? The place where you spend your working life will depend on what you do in retail, but here are just some of the locations you may find yourself in during your working hours.

Positions within Retailing

In a convenience or corner store	Within an inner city shopping mall
In a medium-sized supermarket	In a call centre
In a department store (or concession stand within a department store)	On a ferry, a plane or a train (or in airports, ports and stations)
At head office	Within a huge out-of-town retail park
In an exclusive, luxury designer store	In a DIY centre or in a garden centre
In a market	In a warehouse

IN AND AROUND THE SHOP FLOOR

It's good to bear in mind that 90 per cent of all the staff in retail work in store operations (or store ops) and so there is a very good chance this is where you will begin your career in retail – somewhere within or around the store – even if this isn't where you finally end up!

Sales Staff

Once perceived as rather low on the pecking order, good sales staff are actually vital to the success of any business. This is because they provide the human face of retailing. They are the bridge between the public and the company they work for and good, efficient, polite sales staff are more likely to make customers come back to your shop or store than individuals who are sullen, ill-informed and can't be bothered. Sales staff include sales assistants. These are the people who remain on the shop floor replenishing shelves or rails, returning unwanted goods to their correct sector, directing customers to specific areas of the shop, and helping to pack bags and take purchases to the customers' cars. They may also be responsible for marking up reductions (especially during the sales) and putting up the new season's promotional material. They include retail cashiers and checkout operators, whose job has been revolutionised by the advent of new technology. Where once their responsibility was simply to take payment for goods and provide the correct change, these days they may also be handing out cashback, dealing with credit cards, handling both Euros and pounds and also making sure customers are using their store loyalty cards.

Call Centre Operatives

In mail-order businesses, and to a lesser extent click and mortar businesses where there is no face-to-face contact between the customer and retailer, the role of call centre operative is very important. They are the voice, if not the face, of the company and when people ring in to place orders or to query a non-delivery, a payment or a price, the operative must be able to deal with the enquiry quickly and positively. They must be able to think on their feet and remain polite and patient at all times, even when the customer isn't right! They also need good keyboard skills as they will be entering all the variables on a customer's order (size, colour, quantity, delivery date etc) into the main computer. Once again, if they do their job properly the company is more likely to get return business from its customers and a happy customer means more sales.

Produce Assistants

In supermarkets and food stores generally (butchers, greengrocers, fishmongers) you will find produce assistants. They are responsible for making sure out-of-date items or damaged goods are removed from the shelves, that the display looks attractive to the customer and that everything is properly labelled and priced. They may have to move stock if there is a special offer on and check with stock control if certain goods are not coming down the supply line quickly enough. As with all members of the sales staff, they really have to have good knowledge of what the store actually stocks, what the product actually is and what it looks like. For instance, produce assistants in the greengrocery section are given specific training so they can recognise what all the different fruit and vegetables such as okra and kumquats actually look like. In butchery and fishmongery they will be trained to de bone meat or fish and to advise customers on the best cut of beef or type of shellfish to use for different recipes. All produce assistants must have a first class knowledge of health and safety, not only in order to protect the public from food infections such as salmonella and listeria, but also to protect themselves from injury from the razor-sharp knives and slicers they use every day.

Personal Shopper

As people's lives become increasingly stressed the role of personal shopper becomes more important. Many people are now cash rich but time poor, they simply cannot spend hours browsing through a store looking for their perfect purchases. This is where the personal shopper comes in. He or she is usually employed by a large department store and their job is to know the store's stock inside out. They build up a relationship with a customer, finding out their personal preferences, and then choose items they think are ideally suited to that customer. They could be looking for anything from a special outfit for a wedding to Christmas presents for members of their client's family. Personal shoppers must have exceptional social skills, be very discreet, and also be alert to new trends and fashions coming through.

Customer Services

Another area where social skills are of paramount importance is in customer services. Customers have always had queries and complaints that customer services have had to sort out, but their role is now much bigger as stores have introduced new services to ensure customer loyalty. Now customer services can arrange a personal shopper for you, they can organise electric scooters and wheelchairs or other mobility vehicles for customers, they can also organise delivery to your door. In large department stores they can check the availability of certain items via their central computer system and track down that very last size 10 dress that just happens to be in their sister store in Aberdeen while the customer is in Bristol. They can even arrange for it to be transported to the customer's home store via their nationwide distribution service. Sorting out refunds, getting points added to customer loyalty cards, arranging financial services such as loans, and exchanging faulty goods are all part of a day's work for customer services and so obviously, communication is of vital importance here. You also have to be able to stay calm under pressure and not lose your temper when things do go wrong. For instance, in fashion outlets during the sales, many people buy multiple items, get them home and then decide they don't like them, or if they are buying for other members of their families, discover they are not the right size. This means the returns desk can become overwhelmed with frantic customers wanting either refunds or exchanges and tempers can get frayed. It is up to customer services to sort out each customer's requirements successfully and to keep the queues moving along, ensuring the customers leave satisfied.

Display Staff

This is one of the more creative sides of the industry and as such it attracts a lot of people and so competition for jobs in display is quite healthy. Positions include visual display assistant, window dresser, or display manager or (display) merchandiser. They take responsibility for all the in-store displays as well as the all important window displays that attract the customers into the store in the first place. Displays have always been changed in conjunction with the arrival of the new season's goods so customers can get a taste of what is new around the store, and it is not unheard of for displays to be changed on a weekly basis, just to keep them one step ahead of the competition.

Display staff in the larger stores usually follow guidelines handed down from head office as to colours and themes, but must then use their imagination and creative talents to produce displays that really entice customers in. They will also be responsible for the upkeep and cleanliness of the displays. (One famous Christmas display for a large London store had the theme 'Cornucopia' and featured a fountain spraying red wine. Unfortunately, the heat of the lights caused the wine to ferment and foam, and so the display manager was forced to find a product that could be mixed with the wine and stop the foaming before the display was ruined.) Many experienced display staff leave full-time employment and prefer to work on a freelance basis.

BACK ROOM BOYS AND GIRLS

Stockroom Staff

The retail staff you don't normally see on the shop floor are just as important to the retail industry as their more visible counterparts. No large supermarket could exist without the shelf-stackers who replenish stocks, mainly while the stores are closed so they don't get in the way of shoppers. Then there are the stockroom staff. They work behind the scenes unpacking deliveries, sorting them, pricing up certain items and ensuring they are ready to be taken out into the store. You need to be very precise to do this because you will be counting in deliveries and will have to chase up any discrepancies on delivery dockets and purchase orders.

Receiving Supervisor/Warehouse Staff

The receiving supervisor acts as the bridge between the stockroom staff and the staff in the warehouse where goods are stored before travelling to the stores and this part of the retail business is known as distribution (or supply chain). These days most of the retail supply chain is controlled electronically. As each item passes through the tills, the information on its colour and size stored within the barcode is passed on to the central stock control computer and replacement stock is ordered automatically. Smaller businesses may still do this manually by physically counting items of stock. Either way, the receiving supervisor still has an awful lot of paperwork to do, checking and crosschecking when new stock comes in. If the wrong stock is delivered, or the right stock is delivered in a damaged state, the receiving supervisor will have to sort the problem out, ensuring the stock is sent back to the relevant supplier and new deliveries are received at the warehouse. Many of the larger retailers own their own warehouses; smaller retailers tend to use independent warehousing companies.

Transport Staff

The transport staff or delivery staff are those that actually drive the lorries between the warehouses and the stores and they also tend to offload the goods from their vehicles and wheel them into the stores. These days they may also be driving the vans that deliver food orders placed via the internet (such as Waitrose's Ocado service) direct to customers' homes. This is an area that is bound to grow as more and more people order online. It's actually seen as a 'greener' alternative to driving your car to the supermarket to do your shopping. Each Ocado van has the capacity to carry 20 different people's shopping from the store to their homes on one run. This means the carbon emissions from 19 car journeys to and from the supermarket are saved.

Wholesale

Bear in mind that in wholesale (where one business sells to another business that will eventually sell to the consumer e.g. a wholesale fashion house that will buy product in bulk and then sell on smaller amounts to a variety of independent fashion shops or boutiques) many of the roles within retail are replicated. For example, most wholesalers will employ sales staff, stockroom staff, warehouse staff, design staff and distribution staff. This is also true of the larger import/export companies.

DID YOU KNOW?

BBC's Money Programme has branded the Co-op the greenest retailer on the High Street after 10 retailing chains were analysed by research company Trucost. It found the Co-op was overall best for carbon footprint, green packaging and recycling of rubbish. Co-op was also the first supermarket to introduce and promote Fairtrade goods.

HEAD OFFICE/MANAGEMENT

Buyers

If you think buying stuff for a living sounds like a dream come true, think again. Although the role of buyer is perceived as glamorous and high profile, it is also essential, high pressure and hectic. To a certain extent the buyer has ·to second-guess what he or she thinks people will want to buy in the coming months. They evaluate products that are already available and decide which they think will sell best in their stores. This means they have to have a very good idea of where the market is heading. They have to keep an eye on trends and especially on their competitors so they don't get left behind. They also look to the future to make sure they buy what people are going to want to purchase in the coming seasons. They also have to negotiate the best possible price with their suppliers (keeping in mind how much they think their customers will be willing to pay for them. Get this wrong and it can seriously affect profit margins).

If the precise product the buyer wants is not available he or she may order something to be made uniquely for their market and must ensure both the product quality and price. Most buyers specialise in one product area, e.g. ladies' or men's fashion, accessories or home furnishings and they need to have specialist knowledge of their market with an eye on fashions, fads and trends. Because of this they will work closely with the merchandising department, however much of their work will be out of the head office, actually talking to suppliers and there are good opportunities for travel in this role. Many people get into buying by first becoming buyer's clerks who assist the buyers by processing orders, talking with the suppliers and handling samples. (See 'Case Study 1'.)

Designers

Think about most of the goods you buy and you will soon realise the importance of the designer's role. From shoes to clothes, fridges, chairs and patterned fabrics, a designer has been involved in the evolution of that product. Designers must always keep one step ahead of fashions, predicting what people will want to buy in the future. They also have to be practical about what they are designing (they use the term ergonomics – is what they are designing suitable for its intended role? The bottom line is, does it work efficiently?). Most designers study to higher education level and have a degree in design. It is a demanding job but can also be incredibly creative and rewarding.

Food Technologist/Technician

As previously stated, the food technologist is now in high demand as the major food retailers are constantly looking to upgrade recipes and introduce new recipes to entice customers to buy. The company briefs the technologist or technician on what they are specifically looking for (e.g. low fat, low salt foods) and then he or she must create a recipe from scratch, constantly testing it and refining it until the desired flavour/consistency/texture/look is attained. With the government's new healthy eating initiatives in place (such as the green, amber and red food traffic lights system), the job of the food technologist has become even more important. The next big thing for food technologists will be removing E-numbers (artificial colourings and flavourings) from products, especially those aimed at children, while ensuring the food still looks inviting and has good flavour.

Garment Technologist

It is up to the garment technologist to make sure your jeans don't shrink in the wash or the colour doesn't run in your new T-shirt. They test garments for durability and longevity and are constantly sourcing new fabrics to make clothes from. Two new green initiatives are organic cotton and material made from bamboo. The garment technologists at Colorado-based company Crocs – makers of brightly coloured clogs – have now found a way to make shirts, shorts and even skirts out of Croslite, its trademark soft, spongy foam resin. They mix the resin with natural fibres such as cotton and then spin it into a light, breathable yarn. Major fashion companies are crying out for garment technologists, who are in scarce supply as so many people these days do not go on to do sciences (chemistry and physics in particular) at higher education level.

Merchandising

If you can predict a fashion trend (apparently, wedge-heeled shoes enjoyed their five minutes in the spotlight for summer 2007 and stilettos have now made a comeback) then a job in a merchandising department may be just the thing for you. One of the retailer's biggest nightmares is being left with loads of stock nobody wants – that fluorescent green teddy bear for Easter, chocolate truffle stuffing for Christmas. When major retailers get their merchandising forecasts wrong it can have a disastrous effect on sales and profits (this is what happened to Marks & Spencer before its recent resurgence). However, get it right and stock will be flying out of the stores faster than you can restock it. Merchandisers work closely with the buyers to make sure their companies are stocking the perfect range of products to suit their customers. This makes merchandising an exciting place to be but you have to have a good analytical mind to make it in this department because you will be scouring statistics about the market and predicting what is hot and what is not.

Marketing/PR
The merchandiser will rely on information from the marketing department to help them make informed decisions about products. That's because the people in marketing will be out there, talking to customers and looking at press coverage to see what it is people actually want to buy. They gather their information through the media, by conducting customer questionnaires and increasingly by analysing the data stored on customers' loyalty cards, which immediately give them access to an individual's buying patterns (how often you purchase items from the store, how much you spend and even what products you buy). They are also responsible for promoting the products wherever they can, increasing customer awareness. They are responsible for marketing campaigns such as special offer vouchers and advertising in the local and national press.

Similarly, PR is responsible for raising customer awareness of your brands or product. PR departments can be in-house (i.e. based at head office) or independent and will answer any queries or requests from members of the press. They will arrange samples to be sent out for magazine shoots, send out press releases containing new product information, inform the press about upcoming promotional events such as photo opportunities with celebrities and generally keep their company's name in the spotlight. Communication skills and being a real people's person are essential to work in PR.

Both merchandising and PR are very competitive areas with jobs at a premium (mainly because they are seen as being quite glamorous) so you have to work hard and get good grades to gain entry.

IT/Technology

If technology and computers are more your bag then the IT department could be the place for you. If you want to get ahead in retailing you have to have computer skills. You will be dealing with complicated computerised tills on the shop floor; in the stockroom information about the amount of stock coming in and going out is now computerised and nearly every major store worth its salt has its own website. Just think about it, even five years ago almost no one ordered their food over the internet, but nowadays it is commonplace to see minivans from the major supermarkets driving up to people's homes and delivering their groceries straight to their front doors. These orders have been placed over the internet and it is up to the IT departments to constantly update websites and ensure new systems are in place and running efficiently. In fact, IT skills are desirable whatever job you in do in retail as so many systems are now computerised, but if you are an IT whiz, a job in a specialised IT department could see you go far and a lot of the larger retail companies now run graduate IT schemes.

Human Resources

Retail is a cut-throat industry and everyone wants the best people to come and work for them. Also, once they have got the staff they desire, they want to hang on to them for as long as possible. The amount of talent poaching that goes on in the higher echelons of retailing is unbelievable, but keeping hold of staff further down the ladder is just as important. This is because training takes time and money and you don't want to lose one well-trained member of staff only to have to start the process from scratch with someone else. The human resources (HR) department is there to make sure employees are happy and working to their full potential. HR will organise recruitment and training. It will nurture employees' career development plans and talk through any problems such as personality clashes. It will also handle pay and benefits, and oversee (if necessary) any disciplinary procedures, which means people working in this sector must be able to comprehend a mass of employment legislation including racial equality, maternity rights, sickness or disability. This is a job for individuals who have exceptional 'people' skills, who can listen carefully and offer practical solutions to problems.

Management

The further you go up the retail promotional ladder the more responsibility you will have and those that ultimately have the most responsibility are the managers. You will be overseeing not only the stock and the staff but also the stores themselves and their profit margins. You need to be committed, concentrated and keen and the managers who show the most enthusiasm can quickly rise from the lowest levels to the highest. Most start as management trainees, learning the ropes while actually doing the job. Trainees often move around from department to department or different job areas of a business so they can get a good grounding in everything. From here they usually progress to assistant manager, where they have more responsibility but ultimately report to a manager above them.

Within large stores you can become a department sales manager where you are responsible for a specific department such as ladies' fashion, or maybe the electrical department. If you are working for a company with a large number of stores dotted around the country you could become a regional manager where you could have as many as 20 stores in your jurisdiction. Many larger firms provide their own training courses that are a mix of classroom-based teaching and on-the-job experience to develop your leadership and people management skills. You don't need to be a graduate to make it into management in retail, how far you get depends more on your own unique talents and abilities, and it is nice to bear in mind that some people who started out on the shop floor have made it all the way up to managing director. This shows the possibilities for advancement in retail really are as far reaching as you want to make them.

E-commerce Positions

Many of the jobs mentioned above are replicated within e-commerce companies. They may not need sales assistants on the shop floor but they will need sales staff to process customers' orders, customer care employees to deal with queries and complaints, managers, and human resource staff. However, the most important and biggest area of employment within e-commerce is in IT. For a start the company's website has to be designed and maintained and this will need the services of IT consultants, software support staff and hardware engineers. They may also employ a systems analyst or developer. If you are interested in the world of e-commerce you will need excellent computer skills and bear in mind that most of the vacancies in the IT area are at graduate level. For more information on jobs within this sector, have a look at *E-Commerce Uncovered*, published by Trotman and also 'Case Study 2'.

Other Areas

Other areas in retail you might like to consider are becoming a security guard (most large stores now employ their own security operatives), owning/managing your own shop (everything from a patisserie to a boutique), or being a market trader with your own market stall.

By now you should have a better idea of the jobs you can do in retail, but what do you want to do – and more importantly, what are you actually suited to doing? In the following chapter we will be exploring the talents and abilities that will help you get on in some positions and the character traits and physical aspects that may make you unsuitable for others.

DID YOU KNOW?

The famous Hamleys toy store in London's West End is extending its brand by opening stand-alone shops around the country. Although it already has six stores in airports across the country it also plans to open stores in Edinburgh, Glasgow, Manchester and Liverpool. Hamleys has been operating at its store in Regent Street for 250 years.

5

CLAUDIA MIHALACHE

Case study 2

THE E-COMMERCE PRODUCT MANAGER

After gaining three good A-levels at school, Claudia decided to go to university to study for a BSc in International Economics. She soon realised this was not the route she wanted to take so left in order to take a MSc course in Marketing and Management. She really enjoyed it and it led her to her current career path at the Dixons online operation, www.dixons.co.uk.

Here, Claudia is managing to combine her interest in retail with work in the online market, which she feels to be more dynamic. Now 23 years old, Claudia is MDA (major domestic appliances) and SDA (small domestic appliances) E-commerce Product Manager.

'My day-to-day duties involve looking after the online trading for large white goods (such as fridge/freezers, known as MDA) and small white goods (such as toasters,

You need to be confident and quick of the mark. You can't afford to si back and jus be taken fo the ride as this is a very fast-paced industry to work in.

known as SDA) on the internet site. No two days are the same because of the variety of things I have to do, such as ensuring our prices are competitive. I have to check our prices against those of a given set of competitors and then take action if need be. I also manage a number of our campaigns on Google and have to ensure our costs stay below a budgeted level while still increasing our revenue.

'I manage the contents of the website to ensure that everything in the MDA and SDA categories is accompanied by the relevant marketing text and photographs so customers get the best experience online. Sometimes this means contacting the manufacturers to source the best material possible for the site. I regularly have to come up with new promotions to ensure we attract new customers and I have designed a number of web pages that our customers can use to find out more about certain brands we have in stock.

'I love the fact online marketing is ever changing! For example, some days I could be coming up with a new promotion, or coming up with a new web page or new campaigns to support my overall trading. There are some tasks that need to be completed daily, but essentially no two days are the same, which keeps me on my toes. The biggest downside is it's 24/7. This will never be a purely 9 to 5 job as there

DID YOU KNOW?

A new 'catwalk to check-out' chart lists the companies that come out winners in managing to copy catwalk looks the most rapidly and successfully. The top three High Street chains on the list, getting up to 90 per cent of the key womenswear looks in their shops, are Warehouse, Zara and Topshop.

Source: Retail Consultancy Piper-Jaffray.

are times you are required to either work later or come in on weekends to ensure some things get done, like new product launches.

Be enthusiastic and give 110 per cent to everything you do as it will help to further your career within this sector.

'I'm already sure I want to keep working in the online retailing industry as I believe it is the future of retailing. That's why I want to get a CIM qualification (Chartered Institute of Marketing – see the 'Further information' section) as it would undoubtedly be very useful to my role. They are now doing a Diploma in E-commerce, which is something I would definitely like to pursue. But for the moment I'm enjoying the experience I'm gaining at Dixons and want to work hard here so I can progress further in the company.

'I'd say to anyone wanting to do what I do: just be enthusiastic and give 110 per cent to everything you do as it will help further your career within this sector.'

Tools of
the trade

6

Now you will have a better idea of what it is people actually do in retail, but is it for you? This is a business where things move very fast and constantly change so if you like a quiet life you may wish to explore jobs which are less demanding. However, if you have a real passion for retail, like the bustle and the rush you get from meeting new people and doing different things every day, then you could be one of the young, dynamic employees the industry is crying out for.

If you have a real passion for retail, like the bustle and the rush you get from meeting new people and doing different things every day, then you could be one of the young, dynamic employees the industry is crying out for.

Remember, in retail you can move up the promotion ladder extremely quickly, which means pay rises and more professional kudos, but as anyone already in the industry will tell you, you must be really hungry for success in order to get it. In chapter 11, 'Career Opportunities', we will explore just how you go about getting into the industry, but

here we list the personal qualities, attributes and strengths
you can bring to the job that will give you a head start over
rival candidates. The world of retailing doesn't suit
everyone, but this list will help you to make up your mind
whether or not you suit it and it suits you.

Being a People Person

If you are afraid to say boo to a goose you really should
steer clear of retailing because if you can't talk to people
and really communicate with them how are you ever going
to sell them anything? In retail you are interfacing with
people on a daily basis, some of whom you will know, while
others will be total strangers. If you are on the shop floor
you will be dealing with customers, if you are a buyer you
will be talking to suppliers and if you are a manager you will
be talking to staff, customers, buyers, head office and
everyone else involved in the supply chain. People skills can
be learned with experience but if you are a naturally
gregarious, outgoing, friendly person you'll get on in retail
faster than someone who is more reticent.

Good Communication Skills

These lead straight on from being a people person. It's OK
to smile and be friendly and polite, but if no one can
understand what you are on about then you are not going to
get very far. Whoever it is you talk to during the working day
you must ensure they get the gist of what you are saying
quickly and easily so that mistakes don't get made. This is of
equal importance if you are talking on the phone or face to
face; however, if you work in a call centre it becomes even
more important. Customers don't have the time to repeat
everything they tell you down the phone so if they order a
pair of jeans in size 12, long length, they expect you to take

the order correctly and for you to give them information on payment and delivery clearly and efficiently. Beverley Paddey, the Head of Standards and Qualifications at Skillsmart Retail says employers are crying out for candidates with good oral communication skills. 'These days, so many young people spend hours on their computers or texting each other they don't practise actually talking and so their oral skills are not as good as they could be.' Remember, it's good to talk, so make sure your communication skills are excellent.

Be Organised

Customers expect good service when they are out spending their hard-earned cash and if they come across a shop that runs smoothly and gives them what they want hassle-free they will be more inclined to stay loyal to it. This is why you need to be organised. You want the whole selling and buying process to run smoothly. Being organised includes being a good timekeeper because if the shop you work in opens at 8 in the morning, there's no use you breezing in at 8.15 am. Poor timekeeping is disrespectful, giving the impression you don't think much of your job, so buy yourself an alarm clock! Being organised also means making sure you have clean uniforms if you wear one, keeping good records if you are involved in stock takes, and remembering to bring in name badges, keys to the stockroom and the other paraphernalia associated with your job. Having the basics of your working life sorted clearly in your mind will give you breathing space to deal with any problems that are bound to occur during the course of a busy day.

Numerical Skills

Going hand in hand with the organisation of your everyday life is your ability to organise numbers. There are numbers everywhere in retail – from prices and price codes, to giving change and refunds, to stock lists and inventories – so if maths is Martian to you, you may find retailing just as alien. Yes, it's true most of the pricing and selling at the tills is computerised, but if you can remember relevant stock codes or the number of the aisle the bread is in, it is going to make your life easier. Even in the merchandising department you will be analysing statistics, looking at sales figures and getting stuck in with numbers, while buyers will have to decide just how much of a certain product to order. If sums do your head in then retail is really going to give you a headache.

Being IT Literate

Increasingly in our gadget- and gizmo-led world, having good IT skills is essential and this is especially true in an industry like retail where so many areas are governed by computerised systems. Just think about it; every time someone buys a pair of socks in Marks & Spencer or a tin of beans in Tesco, the sale is electronically acknowledged as the barcode is read through the till. This automatically tells the stock control computer how many pairs of socks or tins of beans are now left in store and when levels of stock get really low, more is automatically ordered up from the warehouse. As an employee you will be expected to know how to input information and extract it from the computer systems you encounter not only at the POS (point of sale) and in stock control, but also at head office, in the warehouse and especially while working with e-commerce. So make sure you are computer-savvy, it will really help you to get ahead.

Fit for the Job

Talking of headaches, there are some areas of retail where

having good physical health will really stand you in good stead. If you work in the stock room, warehouse or on the shop floor it is more than likely you will spend a significant part of your working life on your feet and you'll probably be doing a lot of walking. If you are a stockman or a sales assistant you may also find yourself doing a lot of lifting as you unpack new stock, move it around and/or put it out on display. You need to have stamina and strength. Many women sales assistants swear by support tights to help with tired, aching legs after a day on the shop floor!

Be Decisive

As a customer there is nothing worse than going into a store and asking an assistant a question, only for them to look back at you like a startled rabbit and say 'oh, I don't know!' This is not the right answer or the right attitude. You need to be decisive, i.e. make decisions quickly. The correct reply would be more along the lines of 'let me take you to the customer services desk/manager, they will be able to help you straight away!' It would, of course, be even better if you could answer the question yourself, but there are always going to be queries you haven't come across before; however, dithering really isn't an option – make the decision to find out. If your managers can see you are capable of making the right decisions under pressure they are more likely to put you forward for promotion.

If your managers can see you are capable of making the right decisions under pressure they are more likely to put you forward for promotion.

Ability to Cope with Stress

So how stressful can selling a few apples be anyway? The answer is 'very'. Retail moves so fast the demands on you will come as a constant flow. Customers will need your help, head office may be crying out for sales figures, at Christmas products can move out of the store so fast you have to fight to keep shelves and rails stocked. What happens if the automatic doors to the store get jammed shut, or a till goes offline, or a delivery van breaks down? You will have to learn to cope with the stress of working under pressure nearly every day. Having many of the qualities listed above will lower your stress levels simply because they will help you overcome the problems you encounter, but being able to stay calm and think straight are really going to help.

Be Enthusiastic

Whatever else you bring to a job in retailing, enthusiasm will take you the farthest. An eager, smiling employee, willing and able to tackle anything his or her manager throws at them will soon become an invaluable member of staff. Being enthusiastic will really help you progress quickly because so much of what you learn in retailing is learnt on the job. If you take on all the jobs you can you will gain experience across a whole range of retailing positions. Also, showing enthusiasm can inspire those around you to be more enthusiastic – it's a leadership skill that could mark you out for greater things.

Love the Product

One of the best bits of advice for anyone coming into the industry is to know what you like yourself as a consumer. If you are fanatical about music, working in a music store such as HMV is going to suit you more than working at B&Q. If you are a fashion junkie then apply for jobs with fashion houses or boutiques. If beauty products press your buttons then what about working for a beauty franchise such as Clinique in a department store or starting out at a chemist. Later in the book there is a case study with a young golf enthusiast who decided to do his work experience in a Golf Pro Store. Why? Because he loves golf, has experience with different golf clubs and knew he could talk to the customers coming into the store about their shared hobby – golf! You become a better salesperson when you love what you sell and have a deep knowledge of it because customers pick up on your passion.

WORK ON YOUR KEY SKILLS

Beverley Paddey says 'Employers across the industry are crying out for employees who have good key skills. That is why it is so important while still at school to work on these skills, which may seem obvious, but which a surprising number of employees do not have to the necessary level. They include turning up on time, being able to listen, being able to communicate orally, creating empathy and transactional analysis. Having these core key skills will set you ahead of other candidates when you come to get a job in retail.'

THINGS TO CONSIDER

All the above are positive attributes you can bring to a job in retailing, however, there are several things you should take into consideration that may put you off before you even begin.

Antisocial Hours

Many jobs in retail require that you work at weekends and do some late evenings a week. In some areas people will also work overnight (doing big stock takes or restocking the store). It is also more than likely your store will be open on Bank Holidays and over Christmas. If you are not prepared to work antisocial hours you may have to rethink a career in retail.

Physical Disabilities

If you suffer from a physical disability that makes getting around difficult there may be jobs in retail that won't suit you. The same goes for some specific health problems. For example, if you have a family history of back problems then lifting heavy loads in the stock room will not be an ideal job for you. However, many of the bigger retailers actively encourage those with disabilities through special schemes to pinpoint the most suitable positions.

Shyness

You can't be a shrinking violet in retail or as quiet as a mouse – you have to get out there and interact with your work colleagues and with the public – so if being around other people and talking to them all day long gives you the shivers, you'd better think of another career.

Low Pay

It's highly likely your wages will not be very high when you start – this can change quickly as you move up the retail ladder; however, if you are not prepared to put up with low pay when you initially start work in retail, especially if you are on the shop floor, you may like to consider doing something else.

Starting at the Bottom

Even if you are a graduate, you will have to start your career in retail quite low down on the career ladder. This can change quickly but, as Anne Richardson explains, not quickly enough for some people. 'A lot of people who come into the sector want to do managerial jobs immediately without being willing to put the time in on the shop floor,' she says. 'This is really short sighted because you have to learn to walk before you can run. If you bear in mind you could build your whole career in the retail sector, be patient enough to spend those months or years on the shop floor and your commitment will be rewarded.'

Being on Your Feet

If you are working on the shop floor or in a warehouse then it is highly likely you will be on your feet for much of the day. You will probably be doing a lot of walking too – getting stock from the stock room, finding items for customers, returning unwanted stock from the changing rooms. If your idea of the perfect job is sitting behind a desk all day then all this standing and walking probably means a job in retail is not for you.

RETAIL QUIZ

If you still think a career in retail could be for you then the following section is a fun way to see just how much you really know about the industry. Based on things that happen around the shop floor it will test your knowledge of customer care and retail awareness; do you really know what a sales assistant's responsibilities are and if

DID YOU KNOW?

The value of the organic cotton market in Britain surged by 50 per cent in 2007 to £60 million. The growth has been spurred by more High Street stores such as Topshop stocking organic brands such as People Tree.

you did join a retail company would you be a profitable resource? Simply choose the answer you believe is right or is closest to what your own response to a situation would be. And don't worry if you get some wrong, making sure you know the right answers is why all these companies have training schemes!

1. A lady approaches the till at her local supermarket and offloads all the products from her trolley onto the conveyor belt. You're about to relieve the cashier but when you enter your employee code number into the till, the computer starts to shut down. Now the lady is left at a till that isn't working. Do you:

   A. Scream for your line manager, not knowing what else to do?
   B. Explain to the customer what has happened and tell her she is going to have to go to another till?
   C. Explain what has happened, help her to put all her goods back in her trolley and wheel her to the customer services till so she doesn't have to wait in line for one of the ordinary tills to become vacant?

2. Which of the following is the most important reason a store could give for poor sales figures over the Christmas period?

   A. Christmas stock arrived in the store too late to take advantage of the whole Christmas buying period?
   B. Stock was displayed at the wrong places within the store so customers weren't aware of it?
   C. The stock was priced too high so customers were put off buying it?

3. You're in a furniture store call centre and a call comes in from a customer who has just received a table via your delivery van, but the table is damaged and will have to be returned. You check the stock list to discover this is the last table of that type and the brand is about to be discontinued. Do you:

   A. Apologise and suggest the customer choose something else up to the same value as the table as an exchange item?
   B. Explain the situation and ask whether the customer would like an exchange or a full refund and arrange for the van to go back and pick up the damaged goods?
   C. Tell her she can get a refund but the cost of delivery will still be taken from her account?

4. You see a customer take an item off a shelf and hide it under their coat. What should your first action be?

   A. Alert the store security because they are obviously shoplifting?
   B. Go up to the customer and ask them if they would like a basket, or if they would like help with their purchases?
   C. Turn a blind eye?

5. You are working behind the counter at your local newsagent and a lad comes in and asks for a pack of cigarettes. You are not sure how old he is, but think he could be around 16. Should you sell him the cigarettes?

   A. Yes.
   B. No.

6. While you are on the shop floor a customer approaches you with a query about the price of an item. You don't know the price off the top of your head and the item doesn't appear to have a price tag on it. Do you:

   A. Direct the customer to the till saying they will handle it there?
   B. Try and find another member of staff who might know the price?
   C. Go with the customer to the till and check the price yourself?

7. A customer says she has seen a drop-dead skirt in a magazine and that it comes from your store. Unfortunately, your particular branch doesn't appear to stock it. What do you do?

   A. Tell her you've sold out of that item?
   B. Give her the number of head office to ring when she gets home?
   C. Explain that although you don't have it in stock, another branch may well do and offer to go to the customer services desk with her where you can ring head office to see if the skirt can be ordered for her?

8. During a stock check you discover two pairs of shoes are missing. You're pretty sure you checked the delivery from the warehouse correctly, so which of the possible explanations below could account for the discrepancy?

   A. There has been an internal transfer to another store and someone has not filled out the necessary paperwork.

B. A member of staff has stolen them.
C. A customer has stolen them from the display.
D. They were faulty and have been sent back to the manufacturer.

ANSWERS

1.   C. This is based on a real event at a branch of a well-known supermarket. In fact, in reality the cashier told the customer she would have to go and queue at another till. Understandably, the customer was not happy and stormed out leaving her goods unpaid for. She subsequently complained to head office, who sent her £20 worth of 'good will' vouchers to spend in the store. You don't want to upset customers, who may not be willing to come back to a store where they feel they have been badly served, so make sure you do all you can to help them.

2.   All three. According to newspaper reports in January 2004, these are the three reasons why Sainsbury's had disastrous sales over the 2003 Christmas period. By the time seasonal stock turned up in the store many people had already made their Christmas purchases elsewhere, others simply could not find the Christmas stock because it was not displayed prominently enough or wasn't in the right place within the store. There was also the question of price. Many customers thought prices were too high and so decided to shop in other stores where prices were perceived to be better value.

3.   B. Damages are a fact of life in retail and most companies have well worked out procedures for dealing with them. Most companies that make deliveries are more than prepared to pick up damaged goods free of charge and they certainly won't make the customer pay for the initial delivery of a damaged product – they want to retain customers, not drive them away with unreasonable costs.

4. B. It is always best to try and deter possible shoplifters rather than wait until they actually commit the crime and then try and catch them. By offering a basket or your assistance you are alerting the customer to the fact they are under scrutiny and you are also giving them a chance to turn away from the act and go and pay for the item legitimately. If they decline your advances you can then alert a member of security to the situation. You should never, ever turn a blind eye to theft because it affects your company's profits. This can lead to higher prices for customers and affects you directly because it can mean bonuses are cut.

5. B. The government recently raised the age at which individuals can purchase cigarettes from 16 to 18 years old and as a retailer you always have to be aware of legislation. Even if you think the customer could be 16 years old you cannot serve him. In a situation like this you should always ask for some form of ID (like a driving licence) that has a date of birth clearly printed on it.

6. C. Customer service is all in retail and your aim is to be polite and friendly, but above all efficient, so don't pass the buck-deal with the query yourself. By taking the customer to the till you are showing they are personally important to your business. Apparently, one satisfied customer will tell ten people how pleased they have been with your service – that's a lot of good press to generate among potential customers.

7. C. Once again, it is all about customer service. These days inter-store transfers – those between one store and another – are exceptionally easy to handle because most of the work is done via computer. Most head offices not only know exactly how much of a particular item they have in stock, but also in which colours and sizes and in which branches. Many stores now offer a service whereby they will endeavour to order an item and get it to the branch of the customer's choice within 48 hours. Make the customer happy – it's what you are there for.

8. All four. Losses are broken down into two categories: known loss, such as breakages and damaged or faulty stock; and unknown loss such as internal or external theft. This is why stock checks are so important – you need to keep track of where your stock is going. It should, of course, be going out of the front doors paid for by customers. If it is disappearing without payment then it is costing your firm money. As part of the sales team it is up to you to do everything you can to combat loss and protect profits and this means making sure you fill out return forms correctly, being accurate in your stocktakes and keeping an eye on what is happening on the shop floor.

Well done! By now you really should have a good idea of how far your knowledge of the retail business stretches. Now is the time to find out what joining this dynamic industry would mean to you in terms of opportunities to progress and earn a decent living.

7

JONATHAN BARON

Case study 3

THE RECRUITMENT CO-ORDINATOR

Jonathan started his working life at a recruitment agency specialising in finding people for the retail sector.

One of the agency's clients was a chain of computer retailing shops and 29-year-old Jonathan then moved to this company to work in its human resources department. He is now responsible for co-ordinating all of the recruitment for the group including personnel for the head office as well as the sales staff for the stores.

'What I look out for in potential staff is resilience and ambition. Our staff need to be money driven, self-motivated and customer focused. The retail staff work on a commission basis so even though the basic wage is low when they first start, they can make it up as the commission is excellent.

What I look out for in potential staff is resilience and ambition. Our staff need to be money driven, self-motivated and customer focused.

'Most of our training is done on the job but we also have a training suite at head office where all retail staff go through an induction and where they can be brought in for retraining. Once trained the opportunities for progression are really good. Normally in our company people go from being a sales advisor to senior sales advisor and then to assistant manager, store manager, area manager and then head office-based managerial positions.

DID YOU KNOW?

Nearly half the workforce in retail works part-time.

'What I love about what I do and about retail overall is the fact you are facing new challenges every day and there are targets you are aiming for. Reaching them gives you great job satisfaction. Retail can be a job for life, either just on the shop floor selling, or as a long-term career progression up the retail ladder. The computer industry is an ever-growing market and so it is a very healthy area of retail to be in.'

What I love about what I do and about retail overall is the fact you are facing new challenges every day and there are targets you are aiming for.

8

FAQs

You should have a really good sense of what retailing is all about by now, but deciding on the course of your future career is an important and difficult task. You may feel you have the qualities to make a go of it, but what of the wider retailing picture? Does the service industry sector have a bright future and what is in it for you? In what ways could working in retail enhance and improve your life? Below are listed some of the most common questions people joining the retail industry ask. Read the answers carefully because they will really help you to make up your mind if a career in retailing is for you.

Once Qualified, Can I Move up the Promotion Ladder Quickly?

You most certainly can. As stated earlier, it is not unheard of for members of the board and managing directors to be in their late thirties and early forties. The big retail companies are very keen to keep hold of good staff, which is why they try to promote from within. They are also very supportive of members of staff who wish to train further in order to gain promotion (and many run their own in-house training schemes), so if you show a willingness to learn, then the opportunities to progress are good.

Will I be Able to Move into Other Areas?

Certainly. Once you have achieved the required level of training and experience you could move sideways from sales into distribution or even across into buying (see 'Case

Study 1'). In department stores there will be the opportunity
to move between different areas (e.g. interiors, fashions,
electrical goods) within the store. With big companies there
may also be the possibility to relocate to different branches
or to move from a branch or store to head office. You
could also move from the bricks and mortar side of a
business to its e-commerce arm.

What Will my Typical Hours be?

As in most other service industries, there are no typical
hours. Retail outlets need to be open to accommodate
the needs of all their customers and this typically means
at weekends and at least one late night a week (usually
Thursdays) as well as 9am to 5pm (or 8am to 6pm)
during most weekdays. Because of this, people who work
in stores tend to do shift work, working a certain number
of weekend hours and late night hours a month with time
off in lieu. There is also the possibility of earning
increased pay for working extra hours and anti-social
hours including Bank Holidays. Do remember the two
busiest times of the year are during summer sales and
the run up to Christmas and the subsequent
post-Christmas sales, and you may well be asked to work
extra hours at these times. Jobs based at head office
tend to entail ordinary office hours but even here, many
employees work extra hours (buyers will be out and about
talking to suppliers, which may include travelling abroad).
This can make a job in retail tiring, but the hours you put
in will definitely pay off in the long run.

Will I get Time Off for Holidays?

Yes, you will, but they may not be when you traditionally
take them! Once again, the always frantic Christmas

period and annual January and summer sales periods are when the efforts of every member of staff will be needed, so it will be all hands on deck at these times. Average holiday entitlement is between four and five weeks a year depending on whether you work full-time or part-time and who you work for. Bear in mind that many part-time staff are parents (single or otherwise) and may want to take time off during the school holidays, including half-term.

How Much Can I Expect to Earn?

The honest answer is not much to start off with, but with more training come regular pay rises. For instance, the most junior positions pay around £9,000+ per annum, while those entering junior trainee management can earn between £9,000 and £18,000. According to Connexions Direct, a checkout operator usually earns between £7,500 and £11,000, while butchers start on around £10,000 rising to £25,000 for a master butcher. As previously stated, food technologists are in short supply at present and can earn anything from £25,000 to £65,000, while shopkeepers start on approximately £15,000 rising to £30,000. If you have a degree then your starting salary will be higher still. For instance, a new entry graduate can earn a salary of between £20,000 and £25,000. In the 2007 issue of *Target* magazine (supported by Skillsmart Retail) the following employers quoted these salaries for graduates. M&S, between £21,000 and £24,500; Sainsbury's £22,000; Next £17,000 (plus benefits); Co-Op £20,500; ASDA £21,500 and Arcadia Group £17,000 to £22,500. However, very experienced buyers and designers can earn £50,000. You may also get other benefits such as getting your uniform (if you wear one) free of charge, enjoying the benefits of staff discounts (these can be considerable) and a subsidised canteen and, with larger firms, the opportunities to join the company's pension or healthcare schemes. None of these should be sniffed at as they all help boost your financial status. Check out the leading retail recruitment websites to see what jobs and salaries are out there (see the 'Further Information' section).

Will I Be Able to Use My Skills Abroad??

Many people working in retail already do. Many buyers spend time in other countries sourcing new raw materials and/or products for sale into the UK market. Many companies in the UK are actually owned by foreign companies (ASDA is owned by American giant Wal-Mart), or are foreign themselves (Mango hails from Spain) and so British management may find themselves on fact-finding missions to head offices abroad. Some people, such as those who work in the shops on board cruise liners are, in effect, travelling as they are working. Or take MH Alshaya, a retailing operation based in Kuwait that has the rights to operate over 42 international brands (such as Boots, Debenhams and Foot Locker) as franchised shops in 13 countries including Cyprus, Turkey and Russia. It actively recruits British people who want to work in a new environment and develop their career by living and working in different countries. UK citizens have the right to work in any of the other European Union countries and if you are aged between 18 and 28 years old you can join the Young Workers Exchange Programme. This allows you to get some vocational training or work experience in another EU country for a period of time between three weeks and 16 months. Obviously, if you are travelling to countries where English is not the first language it really does help to speak the local language, and if working abroad is your goal then consider doing French, Spanish, German or other foreign language GCSEs.

You will be at the cutting edge of the industry, seeing the new trends and innovations in fashion and interior design coming through the shop before members of the public ever do.

What Can I Expect to Get out of the Industry Personally?

A real buzz of energy and excitement. At busy times you will be rushing around so much you won't know where the hours go. You will be at the cutting edge of the industry, seeing the new trends and innovations in fashion and interior design coming through the shop before members of the public ever do. You will have the opportunity to meet a really broad range of people from many different walks of life and some of them may even become your best friends. Just think, if you have a real love of the specific area you work in (food, electrical goods, beauty products) you'll be surrounded by it and involved in it every day of your working life. This is a young, dynamic industry where things vary from day to day as new stock comes in and seasonal changes are made, so you certainly won't have the time to get bored. But most importantly, you never need to get stuck in a rut in retailing, because the opportunities to keep on training and moving up are open to everyone.

How Will the Wider Public Perceive me?

Once upon a time people working in retail did not have a very respected image. Poor training meant retail turned out ill-prepared, unmotivated staff who did not offer the consumer a very good service. They were also badly paid for their services and many had no idea about the range of jobs on offer in the industry. Nowadays the industry has got its act together; it has had to due to the cut-throat nature of the competition. Modern well-trained staff who know what they are doing and can offer the customer real service have greatly improved the public's perception of the industry. Although we haven't yet got to the American 'have a nice day' mentality of retail and other service staff, these days it is the norm to see smart, polite, smiling staff in our shops and stores.

DID YOU KNOW?

Waitrose is to invest £800 million in 50 new stores opening over the next five years. It currently has 185 outlets but wants the new stores to boost sales to £8 billion over the next ten years.

Eventually, Could I Be My Own Boss?

You most certainly could. Just think of this staggering statistic: small retailers make up 99.8 per cent of the retail industry in the UK. These are the local family butchers on the high street, the little fashion boutiques and gift shops, the independent convenience store at the top of your road and the hardware stores, electrical shops, pottery and glassware and paper shops we all make use of but probably take for granted each and every day of our lives. When Skillsmart Retail asked a group of 14–19 year olds the career they would most like in retailing 45 per cent of them said they would like to set up their own business. Setting up on your own may seem like a scary prospect but it doesn't even take huge amounts of investment to start your own store. What it does take is experience and a real knowledge of the industry, plus luck, flair and a talent for sniffing out what is going to be the next big thing. If you are really serious about starting your own business there are a number of websites that exist just to help you achieve your goal.

- In England there is a network of Business Links (www.businesslink.gov.uk) with information on choosing premises, employing staff and getting finance.

- In Scotland, Business Gateway (www.bgateway.com) aims to support economic development throughout Scotland and offers a one-stop shop for business start-ups.

- In Wales, Business Eye (www.businesseye.co.uk) offers impartial advice with factsheets and links.

- In Northern Ireland the Enterprise Northern Ireland site (www.enterpriseni.com) and Invest NI (www.investni.com) both provide support for business start-ups.

Training

9

The previous chapters should have given you a pretty good idea of whether a career in retailing is for you or not. If you are certain that it is, the next thing you will have to consider is how you enter the industry. Because retailing is such a dynamic and quickly expanding work sector, there are now many ways in which you can get industry-recognised qualifications. These can make your progression easier and faster, and if you are serious about getting to the top of the profession they will definitely help you achieve your goal.

Although it is not essential to have paper qualifications to enter the industry, you will need some qualifications to get on to certain courses. For example, whatever route you decide to take into retail, having GCSEs or Scottish Highers in English and Maths will come in very useful. Bear in mind some college courses do require a minimum of four GCSE passes and higher education institutions generally require two or three A-levels or Advanced Highers.

Getting good grades isn't the only thing you can do while still at school that will improve your chances of getting on in the industry. By far the best thing you can do is to get some experience actually working in a retailing environment (see the work experience case study in chapter 11 'Career Opportunities') Arrange a Saturday or holiday job with a local store. Working part-time in retailing you will quickly acquire skills and knowledge to deal with customers and will get a taste of what really goes on and have the opportunity to watch what the trained members of staff actually do. This will really help you to decide if this is the career for you and if you decide to take a vocational route, such as an Apprenticeship into the industry, prospective employers will be interested to see it included on your personal development plan (PDP).

NEW INITIATIVES

Beverley Paddey, the Head of Standards and Qualifications at Skillsmart Retail, says there are a lot of new initiatives currently coming through that will significantly help to make the UK's retail workforce better trained and equipped in the future. Some are not yet fully on line, but if you are not due to leave school for another two or three years, these could be of interest.

Diplomas

The Diplomas act as an alternative to GCSEs and A-levels and are for people who want a more 'hands on' approach as they combine practical, on-the-job learning with more traditional learning. The diplomas have three levels.

- Level 1 is broadly equivalent to 4/5 GCSEs at grades D–G

- Level 2 is equivalent to 5/6 GCSEs at grades A–C

- Level 3 is equivalent to 3 A-levels.

The Diploma in Retail will not come on stream in England until 2010.

Baccalaureate/Skills for Work/Occupational Studies
Three new schemes that are already up and running are the
Baccalaureate in Wales, the Skills for Work in Scotland and
the Occupational Studies in Northern Ireland.

The Welsh Baccalaureate (Welsh BAC) recognises almost
anything young people do at school or college through a
Core programme of activities, consisting of four
components (Key Skills; Wales, Europe and the World;
Work-related Education; Personal and Social Education)
plus options such as GCSE, VGCSE, NVQ or BTEC. Go to
www.wbq.org.uk for more information.

In Scotland, the new Skills for Work programme,
Intermediate 2, is a short course to give people real
employability skills. The same is true for the Occupational
Studies (entry level and levels 1 and 2) in Northern Ireland.
These are almost like tasters so people can see if Retail is
really for them. Both these courses are roughly equivalent to
the Young Apprenticeship in England. For more information
on Skills for Work go to www.ltscotland.org.uk and for
Occupational Skills www.deni.gov.uk.

Young Apprenticeships
A successful Young Apprenticeship in Retailing is
already up and running. The young apprenticeships
combine traditional education and vocational education
and give pupils work experience in schools so they learn
employability skills such as timekeeping, communication
and transactional analysis.

Young apprenticeships are for Key Stage 4 pupils who
show real motivation and ability. They learn not only in

the classroom, but also in colleges with training providers, and in the workplace. Pupils follow the core National Curriculum subjects and for two days a week they also work towards nationally recognised vocational qualifications (NVQs). For more information on young apprenticeships go to www.vocationallearning .org.uk/youngapprenticeships.

Foundation Degrees

These are primarily for candidates who are already working in the retail area. Delivered in partnership with employers, they are the training programmes for those who really want to progress to become supervisors, junior managers and owner-managers and can be studied part-time, so trainees can continue working while they are learning. Foundation degrees are higher education qualifications set at one level below an honours degree. There were some problems with foundation degrees when they were first introduced because most employers were not keen to have members of their workforce off the shop floor for the periods when they were learning. Now a model with Tesco is being piloted where 20 candidates in Manchester and 20 candidates in London are doing their foundation degrees online. It seems to be working well and Skillsmart Retail hopes the Foundation Degree in Retailing will continue to grow. For more information go to www.foundationdegree.org.uk.

The Fashion Retail Academy

Opening in 2006, the Fashion Retail Academy has now seen its first students graduate. Here you can take qualifications that were designed by the employers themselves to satisfy their needs. The qualifications are:

- Diploma in Fashion Retail level 2

- Diploma in Fashion Retail level 3

They are really designed to equip people for the sales floor, although training does cover buying and merchandising as well. Apparently, the results have been so encouraging these new diplomas are to be rolled out to the other retail Centres of Vocational Excellence (CoVEs) around the country (see the 'Further information' section).

ESTABLISHED TRAINING SCHEMES

Nationally Recognised Vocational Qualifications

Vocational qualifications can be delivered on both a part-time and full-time basis. Most full-time courses last one or two years and consist of a number of modules that cover different aspects of the job. Courses can lead to a BTEC First, National Certificate/Diploma and HNC/HND qualifications. BTEC courses include First Diploma in Retail and BTEC Higher National Certificate & Diploma in Retail Management. Some universities and colleges also offer honours degree courses in retailing and related subjects. In fact, retailing is one of the UK's largest sources of graduate vacancies. A graduate training scheme normally lasts between one and three years.

Buyers usually enter the industry by becoming a buyer's assistant or buyer's clerk or via the degree, BTEC award or HND route. Once in a job most buyers are advised to gain professional qualifications via the Chartered Institute of Purchasing and Supply (CIPS), mainly because it is becoming increasingly difficult to progress without these or equivalent qualifications. CIPS schemes include block release, full-time and distance learning courses. (See the 'Further Information' section.)

Work-related industry recognised qualifications are retail NVQs/SVQs, where you are assessed on a continuous basis and which are awarded at three different levels. For example, City & Guilds offers NVQs in Retail Management, Retail Operations, and Visual Merchandising while Edexcel offers NVQs in Retail Operations, and Distribution & Warehousing Operations. How long it takes you to complete each level will depend on how quickly you complete each unit of work.

- Level 1 is an introduction to the job and ensures you have the basic skills.

- Level 2 is for more skilled workers who already know the basics. With this level you can enter the retailing industry in a junior position such as shop assistant.

- Level 3 is for workers with greater responsibilities who will generally be first line managers supervising other staff or who have particular product knowledge and expertise.

Higher level NVQs/SVQs are available in more generic areas. Level 4 is for those who wish to take on more demanding management roles such as department heads.

NVQs have recently been changed and are much more flexible. Of the six units students have to complete, only one is now mandatory, while the other five are completely free choice. You can choose from lingerie fitting, bakery, butchery, fishmongering and newer units such as maintaining flowers, petrol station forecourts, mobile phone selling, tea rooms and selling beauty products.

Apprenticeships

Apprenticeship programmes are usually run by the employer, or by an organisation in conjunction with the employer to provide both training on the job, which is supervised by a specialist, and training off the job on the employer's premises, at a college or training centre (either day or block release, or one or two evenings a week). The length of the programme varies from a few months to about two years. Many of the larger firms, such as Marks & Spencer, Tesco and Selfridges run their own industry-recognised training programmes, giving you the chance to earn as you learn. The employer benefits because new staff are getting trained to its own specifications, making it much easier to recruit and promote from within the organisation. The benefits to you are the fact you are actually employed and earning wages, and the qualifications you attain improve your career prospects and your job security. The training offered by such companies is also recognised and valued by other retailers. According to Beverley Paddey, retail is in the top ten of sectors running apprenticeships in terms of numbers of apprentices being trained.

DID YOU KNOW?

In 2007 Taiwanese firm Acer bought computer company Gateway to become the world's third biggest computer manufacturer after Hewlett-Packard and Dell. Acer will now have the potential to sell a staggering 20 million computers annually.

There are two main levels to the Modern Apprenticeship programme.

- Apprenticeship (FMA in Wales or Skillseekers in Scotland). This is based on the NVQ or SVQ level 2 and because you are working at the same time as learning it usually takes about 12 months to complete. The apprenticeship also includes Key Skills in Communication and Number as well as vocationally relevant qualification.

- Advanced Apprenticeship (AAM in Wales or MA in Scotland). An advanced apprenticeship is based on NVQ or SVQ level 3 and normally takes between 15 months and two years to complete. In Scotland the MA also includes five Core Skills and in England and Wales the advanced apprenticeship includes Key Skills and a vocationally relevant qualification.

Apprenticeships are really aimed at school leavers and young people between the ages of 16 and 24 years old. You could be eligible for funding providing you start your apprenticeships by the age of 25.

Information on who to contact for these courses is contained in the 'Further information' chapter.

As anyone who ever turns on the TV these days knows, retailing is big business, from showing people 'what not to wear', to what to buy to make your home and garden more attractive. There are numerous magazines and books out there covering most sectors of retailing. Show your interest by either buying magazines or borrowing books from the library. Keep up with the latest clothing and home fashions by watching those shows on TV. Also read the local papers as they will have news stories on new stores/shopping malls opening in your area and you will be able to find out if they have any trainee places available by contacting them direct or by talking to your careers teacher or advisor.

Show your interest by either buying magazines or borrowing books from the library.

Across the country, there are now 13 Centres of Vocational Excellence (CoVE) in retail. The London College of Communication and the Fashion Retail Academy are both CoVEs for the retailing industry in London. You should ask your careers teacher or officer if there is a CoVE for retailing in your area. Alternatively, check out the Skillsmart Retail website. You should also check to see what courses are actually available to you. As you will now realise there are numerous different options – ranging from courses for shop assistants to store management – so you need to know what is available and what you will be able to apply for. Once again, your careers teacher should be able to advise you, or check the websites of the main awarders of vocational qualifications that are contained in the 'Further information' section of this book to see what courses best suit your needs and abilities. Also, look at the websites of the well-known retailers – they provide lots of information on careers in their stores (see 'Further information').

Battle of the Supermarkets

The supermarket sector is one of the most cut-throat in the whole of retailing with price cutting wars, loyalty cards and new branding all trying to lure customers away from one store to another. While the total spend in the UK's supermarkets is now in excess of £115 billion, the four main supermarket chains account for three quarters of that market. The percentage breakdown is:

TESCO	29.8%
ASDA	16.5%
SAINSBURY'S	15.9%
MORRISONS	12.2%

Opposite is an easy-to-follow guide summarising all the information contained in this chapter, from entry level right up to the most senior positions.

access to

NO QUALIFICATIONS

ENTRY LEVEL QUALIFICATION

FOUR GCSEs (A-D)
GNVQ/GSNVQ level 1
Young Apprenticeship/Retail Diploma/Baccalaureate
selection interview

ON-THE-JOB TRAINING

APPRENTICESHIP ✦ TRAINEE SCHEMES

APPRENTICESHIP (England) **SKILLSEEKERS** (Scotland) **MODERN APPRENTICESHIP** (NI) **APPRENTICESHIP** (Wales)	Industry schemes e.g. ASDA SAINSBURY'S ARCADIA GROUP

e.g.
**SHELF-FILLER
SALES ASSISTANT
WAREHOUSE STAFF
DRIVER
DRIVER'S MATE**

CREDITS/FURTHER LEARNING

ON-THE-JOB QUALIFICATIONS ✦ PROFESSIONAL BODIES

NVQ/SNVQ **BTEC HNC/HND** **FOUNDATION DEGREE** Full-time/part-time/distance learning	Chartered Institute of Purchasing and Supply (CIPS)

CAREER OPPORTUNITIES

DEVELOPMENT OPTIONS

HIGHER EDUCATION ✦ MANAGEMENT ✦ OPEN OWN BUSINESS

10

SARAH WELSH

Case study 4

A DAY IN THE LIFE OF A SALES ASSISTANT

Single mum Sarah Welsh has worked part-time at the Hedge End out-of-town store Marks & Spencer for the last five years.

This large, two storey building consists of a food department, homewear, menswear, children's department, ladieswear, lingerie, cosmetics, Autograph, Per Una, and a Café Marks. Sarah works exclusively on ladieswear although she quite frequently swaps between departments (she has just moved from the 'plus' department for larger women to coats). Her title is Customer Assistant.

'I'm on the shop floor all of the time and I'm just constantly running around. I do a six-hour day from 9am to 3pm and the only time I sit down is my 15-minute break at 11 o'clock so I'm

What I like best about the job is interacting with the customers and also the interaction with other members of staff, they're great!

basically standing all day (we even stand when we are on the tills). On days when you do a four-hour shift you don't get a break at all.

'Our busiest times are Saturdays and Sundays of course, but also between 11am and 3pm when the children are at school. At 3pm it slacks off because people go off to do the school run. Other busy times are the sales and Christmas and one weekend we suddenly became manic in ladieswear because it was the first nice sunny Saturday of the year and everyone was coming in to buy new, lightweight summer clothes.

'Last Saturday I did two 2-hour stints on the till and I also did a stint in the ladies' fitting

> **DID YOU KNOW?**
>
> The new Terminal Five building at London's Heathrow Airport contains 150 retail stores, many of which have never been seen at an airport before. These include luxury gift and jewellery store Tiffany's.

rooms. On another day I may also do some time on the customer service desk. There's not really a lot that can go wrong when you are on the tills because everything these days is computerised – it even tells you how much change to give. However, it is very rare for us to deal with cash or cheques, maybe only one transaction in ten will be cash while you might go a whole day and not see a cheque. Because of this at our store our till discrepancies are really low – something like one pence in every £100. The bulk of what we deal with on the tills is either credit cards or store cards, but mainly debit cards. At the moment I am being trained to be a till controller – that entails making sure people are at the right tills at the right time, that changeovers go smoothly, and dealing with any queries the till staff might have.

'When we work in the fitting rooms we have to check the number of items in and the number of items out, put them on the rail and, depending on how busy we are, give assistance to customers who have queries. My main duties when I am on the customer service desk are dealing with returned items and customer orders because this is where people make the orders and also where they come to pick up orders once they have been delivered to the store.

'What I like best about the job is interacting with the customers and also the interaction with other members of staff, they're all great! The downsides are the antisocial hours (I work alternate Saturdays) and the fact we work very, very hard and it is incredibly tiring. At busy times we have as many as 39 people working in the ladieswear section alone. However, we do get other benefits. I get 20 per cent staff discount on goods and there is also a staff canteen where I'll go to have a sandwich and a drink on my break, and we have a wastage shop where we can buy discounted food when it is about to go out of date. We also get our uniform for free and I get a Christmas bonus, and there's a pension scheme that I am a part of.

'I'm happy with where I am at the moment but there are opportunities to move up to line manager and you also have the opportunity to transfer to other departments within the store if you want to. You need to have people skills to do what I do, you need to be polite and pleasant and be able to deal with people and it is ideal for single parents like me because of the flexibility of the hours I work.'

11

Career opportunities

If, by this stage of the book, you really have decided that retailing is for you, then the next course of action will be choosing what area of retail you want to enter, and also doing your utmost to make yourself the ideal candidate for the job.

Let's look at the different areas first.

● If you are **outgoing** and **sociable with good people skills**.

These will all make you perfect as a member of the sales team. You will be talking to members of the public, answering their queries as well as serving them and generally interacting with others throughout your working day. Your social skills would also come in useful for talking to people on the phone as a call centre operative.

● If you like **travelling** around and **driving**, with a job where you visit various different locations during the day.

A job driving a large delivery truck between the store and the warehouse, or driving a home delivery van between the warehouse or store and customers' houses would suit you. Bear in mind many drivers these days load and unload their own vehicles so you need to be quite physically healthy to do this job.

● If you like **making things**, are good at **art** and always looking out for new fashion trends.

Your interests and skills will make you ideal for joining a design department and eventually becoming a designer. The UK is becoming ever more design conscious and whether you design coffee cups or clothing, much of the retail trade is dependent on what concepts and designs your imagination can come up with. You would also make a good candidate for visual marketing, where your creative talents could be used to increase sales.

● If you like working with **numbers** and are good at **mathematics** and anything involving logistics.

A job in the buying department, the accounts department, or the merchandising department would suit you to a tee. In all three you will be dealing with sales figures, sales projections and statistics.

● If you are **patient** and understanding and like **solving problems**.

The customer services department is crying out for your skills. With diplomacy and tact you will be able to deal with everything from irate customers whose orders haven't arrived, to the new customer who wants to join your company's credit card scheme.

● If you like **technology** and **computers**.

Retail companies are crying out for people with IT skills, especially as e-tailing is set to grow at such a huge rate. You can use your skills to set up websites and update existing websites, design e-advertising and help deliver the day-to-day needs of the IT division.

● If you like to be in charge, can handle a lot of **responsibility** and are **ambitious**.

Then you really should be heading into management. Here, the onus is on you to get things right and you will be responsible for those under your supervision. The stress related to management positions may be higher than in more lowly positions, but so too are the rewards. Once in management there are real opportunities to progress up the career ladder. Just think, you could eventually be managing director of the whole firm. Alternatively, you could decide to go it alone and become your own boss by opening your own store or shop.

HOW TO MAKE YOURSELF STAND OUT FROM THE CROWD

Get Experience

Get yourself a Saturday job in a shop, be it on the counter of your local chemist or the till of a big superstore. Many large retail firms have their own work experience schemes. This is by far and away the best method of discovering whether retail really is for you. Look out for job vacancies in the local press or apply personally to stores and shops.

WORK EXPERIENCE CASE STUDY

16-year-old Paul Christopher has always been a keen golfer and so in June 2005, when it was time for him to do his work experience as part of the school curriculum, he applied to the Golf Pro Shop at his local club, the County Golf Club, Hampshire. They took him on for the whole two weeks of his work experience, in which time he was involved in selling the full range of goods in the shop, including golf clubs, clothing, golf balls, accessories, drinks and confectionery. 'I had to learn to use the till and how they operated the phones and I was selling to members of the public every day,' he recalls. The manager of the shop was so pleased with his performance they asked him to come in over the summer holiday to continue working as they were short staffed.

From here, Paul took on Saturday and Sunday duties, gradually taking on more responsibility as he became more experienced. 'They started to leave me looking after the shop alone for longer periods,' he says. 'Soon, they knew they could leave me to run the shop by myself all day and from here I started to open the shop up by myself in the morning, cash the till and lock up at the end of the day. Now I'm even earning commission on everything I sell.' Even though Paul does not want to go into retail when he leaves college he says it has been the most brilliant experience for him and he has learnt a lot. 'I'm very glad I have

done this because now I know how a shop operates and how a business actually works and
I've been given a lot of responsibility. It has improved my people skills, my communication skills, I'm more organised, and my confidence is now much greater.'

Hone Your Communication Skills

Paul is proof that communication skills are vital for a role in retail. Talk to as many different people as you can. Don't just talk to people of your own age, but chat to older and younger people as well and it definitely helps to talk to people outside of your normal group of friends and family. In retail you will be talking to people from every different walk of life, so the sooner you get used to communicating with them, the better.

Keep Your School Grades Up

Although qualifications are not necessary for all jobs in retail, if you have a certain number of GCSEs it will definitely increase your chances of moving on quickly. On many college courses you will need four GCSE passes to be accepted, while in higher education the criteria is two or three A-levels or Scottish Highers.

Be Interested

One of the best ways to show you are interested is to go out and window-shop: what does Mango have in stock at the moment? How does Dixons display its stock? What seasonal produce does Tesco have in store? Paul did

exactly the right thing by deciding to do work experience
in an area he loved – in his case golf – because he knew
he could chat to the customers about all the golfing
equipment on sale at the Golf Pro Shop. Also, read
mail-order catalogues (have a look through the Argos or
Freeman's catalogues) and see what consumer trends are
being talked about in magazines. If you've made up your
mind what area of the trade you wish to join, then read
the specialist publications concerning that area. These are
widely available (see 'Further information' section).

Be Enthusiastic

No one expects you to know everything at the beginning of
your career, but if you see each new challenge as
something exciting that will further your promotional
prospects rather than as something to be feared you will
progress quickly. Be the first to put your hand up when
managers are asking for volunteers, do tasks willingly and
don't shirk work.

Pay Attention to Your Personal Appearance

Being smart and clean will make you a better prospective
candidate for any job, but for those where you will be
dealing with the public this is especially true. If you don't
wear a uniform make sure your clothing is appropriate for
the store you work within (although you may get away with
jeans and T-shirt in a record store, they may not go down
so well in an upmarket clothes store). If you do wear a
uniform make sure it is clean and that you look tidy. Many
companies supply uniforms free of charge, give their staff a
clothing allowance or, if they are a clothing firm, substantial
staff discount, so make use of it.

Smile!

It's amazing how welcoming a smiling face can be. When you smile you are saying to people 'come and talk to me, I'll be able to help you'. You are also saying 'I'm a confident person' and people will be more willing to trust the judgement of a confident person, even if it is only as far as to tell them whether those shoes suit them or not!

Love Retail!

If you have decided this is really what you want to do with your life then learn to love the industry. This doesn't just apply to your own specific area but the whole of the retail trade. Every major newspaper has daily coverage of the trade within its Business pages. Here you will find out which stores are doing well, whose stock is going down, what the underlying trends are and also the future predictions. Make sure you read these pages. If you decide to move around within retail then these will give you the indicators you need to get jobs with the best companies and those with the brightest prospects.

DID YOU KNOW?

In early 2007 many business analysts were predicting High Street giant Bhs would go bust after a steep upward turn in profits at M&S. However, Bhs boss Sir Philip Green held his nerve and profits rose by 3 per cent to £50 million, mainly due to the refurbishment of many of the company's 185 stores.

You can really fly high when you enter the world of retail. As you gain more experience and work your way up the career ladder you will discover what you like about it the most and will be able to make informed choices about where you eventually want to end up. The diagram below shows what you could be doing as you become better

CAREER OPPORTUNITIES

BASIC TRAINING NVQ LEVEL 1 RETAIL DIPLOMA/YOUNG APPRENTICESHIP

BASIC INTRODUCTORY SKILLS ✦ SALES ASSISTANT/SHELF-STACKER/ CHECKOUT OPERATIVE

MORE TRAINING NVQ LEVELS 2 AND 3/APPRENTICESHIPS

MORE SKILLS AND EXPERIENCE ✦ FIRST LINE MANAGER/SUPERVISOR/ BUYERS ASSISTANT

MORE TRAINING FOUNDATION DEGREE/NVQ LEVEL 4/HIGHER EDUCATION

DEPARTMENT MANAGER/BUYER/DESIGNER/HEAD OF MARKETING/ MANAGING DIRECTOR

12

The last word

By now you should be raring to set yourself loose on the fast-moving, ever-expanding retail industry. Having suffered a mini-recession at the beginning and middle of the 1990s when many high streets became ghost towns of closed stores, retail is booming again. It seems people's need to go out and buy is unstoppable and this means the need to find people to sell to them will continue to grow.

Now is a brilliant time to enter the industry because the retail sector as a whole is finally getting its act together and coming up with well-structured and well-defined training schemes that will give you the experience you need in order to succeed. Listed below are just some of the ways people in retail are training these days.

- Formal training courses – at colleges, either day release or evening release

- On-the-job training – with an external or internal training provider

- Buddying – where a senior member of staff becomes your buddy and shows you the ropes

- Seminars – where guest speakers from the industry will talk about certain aspects of it

- Workshops – where you usually deal with a specific subject, e.g. new technology

- Online, books and video learning.

A job in retail really can be for life and for those with the fire, the drive and ambition it can be both financially and personally rewarding. As part of a successful team you will have the satisfaction of seeing your company grow and become more profitable. If you are on a bonus scheme you will feel the benefit of that profit in your own pocket and as you become more experienced you will be able to choose the job and the company for you. There are no shortages of job vacancies in retail (check out some of the recruitment websites in 'Further information') so this can be a very steady source of employment and how far you want to take it will very much depend on your own ambitions. Hopefully this book will have given you some indication of what retail is all about and what your role in this industry could be.

DO YOU LIKE MEETING LOTS OF NEW AND DIFFERENT PEOPLE?

☐ YES
☐ NO

DO YOU CONSIDER YOURSELF TO BE SENSIBLE AND RESPONSIBLE?

☐ YES
☐ NO

DO YOU HAVE GOOD COMMUNICATION SKILLS?

☐ YES
☐ NO

DO YOU HAVE DRIVE AND ENTHUSIASM?

☐ YES
☐ NO

CAN YOU THINK ON YOUR FEET AND MAKE DECISIONS UNDER PRESSURE?

☐ YES
☐ NO

ARE YOU A SELF-STARTER, ABLE TO TAKE CONTROL?

☐ YES
☐ NO

DO YOU LIKE FINDING OUT ABOUT NEW PRODUCTS?

☐ YES
☐ NO

If you answered 'YES' to all these questions then
CONGRATULATIONS! YOU'VE CHOSEN THE RIGHT CAREER!
If you answered 'NO' to any of these questions then this may not be the career for you. However, you may like to consider some of the other careers mentioned here such as warehouse assistant, stockroom staff or transport staff.

Further information

13

Industry Bodies

The British Retail Consortium
21 Dartmouth Street
London
SW1H 9BP
Tel: 020 7854 8900
Website: www.brc.org.uk

The British Retail Consortium is the lead trade association for retailers, from the big department stores right down to independents. You can find information on news, parliamentary issues and retail statistics on its website. However, if you want detailed information on courses and careers, you should contact Skillsmart.

Skillsmart Retail
Helpline: 0800 093 5001
Website: www.skillsmart.com

This is the Sector Skills Council for the retail sector. Skillsmart has teamed up with Learndirect to establish a retail-specific helpline that provides help, advice and guidance. It also produces a magazine called *Retail Therapy* full of news, case studies and advice. You should be able to get this from your school or your careers advisor, otherwise contact Skillsmart direct.

Chartered Institute of Purchasing and Supply
Easton House
Easton on the Hill
Stamford
Lincolnshire
PE9 3NZ
Tel: 01780 756777
Website: www.cips.org

CIPS is an international organisation serving the purchasing and supply services. It currently has 17,000 members worldwide studying for its qualifications. The start point for qualifications is the CIPS certificate and advanced certificate and you can go on to take the CIPS graduate diploma. Detailed information on registration and qualifications is contained on the website.

Chartered Institute of Marketing (CIM)
Tel: 01628 427120 (advice line)
Website: www.cim.co.uk
Email: qualifications@cim.co.uk

The CIM is the leading international body for marketing and business development. Every year it helps 50,000 people with training and qualifications – everything from its Certificate in Sales up to Professional Postgraduate Diploma in Marketing. If you feel a career in marketing is for you, then check out the excellent website that can help you decide which level to apply for.

Government and Awarding Bodies

Connexions
Website: www.connexions-direct.com

Connexions is aimed primarily at 13 to 19-year-olds and gives excellent information on jobs and careers. In the Career Zone section the Career Bank can offer you detailed information on getting into retail as well as links to related careers in the sector, including food technician and fashion designer.

Department for Children Schools and Families (DCSF)
Website: www.dcsf.gov.uk

If you are undertaking a vocational training course lasting up to two years (with up to one year's practical work experience if it is part of the course), you may be eligible for a Career Development Loan. These are available for full-time, part-time and distance learning courses and applicants can be employed, self-employed or unemployed. DfES also has a list of Centres of Vocational Excellence in Retail around the country.

City & Guilds
1 Giltspur Street
London
EC1A 9DD
Tel: 020 7294 2468
Website: www.cityandguilds.com

The leading provider of vocational qualifications in the UK, City & Guilds currently offers GNVQs and National Awards and National Diplomas in Retail as well as Retail and

City&
Guilds

SORT IT OUT!

HOW DO I KNOW WHICH JOBS
ARE RIGHT FOR ME?

No problem, you can log onto **cityandguilds.com/myperfectjob**
and take 20 minutes to answer a range of online questions which
looks at your interests, personality and lifestyle and suggests job
areas which may suit you. Get all the information on job options,
how to get started and where you can go to study.
cityandguilds.com/myperfectjob

Distributive Services. Look at the excellent website, where you can find exactly what is on offer under Retail and Distribution.

Edexcel
One90 High Holborn
London
WC1 7BB
Tel: 0870 240 9800
Website: www.edexcel.org.uk

Edexcel is responsible for BTEC qualifications, including BTEC First Diplomas and BTEC National Diplomas and Higher Nationals (HNC and HND). The website includes qualification quicklinks. BTEC qualifications in this field include Retail Management (vocational), Retail Operations (NVQ), Retailing (IVQ) and Visual Merchandising (NVQ).

Learndirect
Tel: 0800 100 900
Website: www.learndirect.co.uk

This free helpline and website can give you impartial information about learning.

Learning and Skills Council (LSC)
Apprenticeship Helpline
Tel: 0800 015 0600
Website: apprenticeships.co.uk

Launched in 2001, Learning and Skills Council now has a main office in Coventry and nine others across the country and is responsible for the largest investment in post-16 education and training in England. If you wish to do an apprenticeship, this should be your first port of call as it has specialised information.

For MAs in Scotland you should look at: www.modernapprenticeships.com or www.careers.scotland.org.uk

For MAs in Wales you should look at: www.beskilled.net

Specialist Schools

The Fashion Retail Academy
15–17 Gresse Street
London
W1T 1QL
Tel: 020 7307 2345
Website: www.fashionretailacademy.ac.uk

The Fashion Retail Academy provides a unique combination of retail business and fashion education aiming to introduce students to all of the practical and vocational skills needed for the challenging world of fashion retail. Teaching is a unique collaboration between college and industry staff, through work placements and industry master classes.

Courses offered are Level 2 Diploma in Fashion Retail and Level 3 Diploma in Fashion Retail.

Industry Schemes

Arcadia Group Ltd
Training Programmes Department
10 Great Castle Street
London
W1 8LT
Training Programmes Team: 020 7927 7676
Website: www.arcadiagroup.co.uk/recruitment

You may not know the name, but Arcadia is the largest
fashion retailer in the UK, with over 28,000 employees and
2,300 outlets. The group includes such well-known brands
as Burton, Dorothy Perkins, Evans, Miss Selfridge, Topshop
and Wallis. It has its own Management Training Programme
(MTP). It also has entry-level positions in distribution,
merchandising or buying as well as other vacancies.

ASDA
Website: www.asda.co.uk
Graduate website: www.asdagraduate.com

For information on general vacancies go to the main Asda
website. For detailed information on Asda's graduate
programme go to the graduate website.

Marks & Spencer
Website: www.marksandspencer.com

Student Support
Website: www.marksandspencer.com/studentsupport

Marks & Spencer has a number of training programmes that you may be interested to join. For instance, its Marks & Start scheme launched in February 2004 with work experience placements given to those with disabilities, the young unemployed and those affected by homelessness. Another strand of the scheme is student support that is aimed at talented students who are the first in their family to go into higher education. Every year 35 students are encouraged to go to university with Marks & Spencer providing financial support plus the opportunity to work in a Marks & Spencer store during the holidays and weekends to gain practical experience. This is aimed at students who wish to go into management.

Morrisons
Website: www.morrisons.co.uk

If you click onto 'Our Company' you will find the 'Working With Morrisons' section at the bottom of the page where you can read about all of Morrisons' vacancies, including those in its distribution sector. It also has a fast-track graduate programme.

Sainsbury's
Website: www.sainsburys.co.uk/aboutus/recruitment

At this website you will find a vacancies section which includes graduate vacancies. Sainsbury's has a workforce of over 150,000 across 700 stores.

Tesco
Website: www.tesco.com

Click onto 'Careers' for information on job training and recruitment. Tesco is about to launch a brand new site for young school leavers but you can register here, at the existing site, to get information on Tesco's two training programmes, including the Store Management Programme.

Publications and Periodicals

The Appointment
Website: www.theappointment.co.uk

This twice-monthly magazine focuses on news and developments in both the retail and leisure industries. Features include profiles of leading retailers.

Convenience Store
Broadfield Park
Brighton Road
Pease Pottage
Crawley
RH11 9RT
Tel: 01293 610218
Website: www.william-reed.co.uk

One of many retail magazines published by William Reed (see the website for all of them), the brand leader in the food and drink market. This gives news on the 'corner shop' market and is fortnightly.

Draper's Record
The fashion industry bible, this weekly publication is aimed at retailers and their suppliers and includes trends, news

items, business articles and anything else concerned with fashion.

The Grocer
Broadfield Park
Brighton Road
Pease Pottage
Crawley
RH11 9RT
Tel: 01293 613400
Website: www.grocertoday.co.uk

This weekly publication has news and views about all aspects of the grocery trade.

Multiple Buyer & Retailer
Broadfield Park
Brighton Road
Pease Pottage
Crawley
RH11 9RT
Tel: 01293 846583
Website: www.william-reed.co.uk

This monthly magazine is read by retail buyers and store managers to get news on marketing, new products and business issues.

Retail Therapy
(See under British Retail Consortium/Skillsmart on page 90)

Retail Week
Greater London House
Hampstead Road
London
NW1 7EJ
Tel: 020 7728 5000
Website: www.retail-week.com

Aimed firmly at the large retail market, this weekly magazine has information on all aspects of retail.

Scottish Local Retailer (SLR)
2nd floor Waterloo Chambers
19 Waterloo Street
Glasgow
G2 6AY
Tel: 0141 222 5384
Website: www.william-reed.co.uk

Covering the whole of Scotland, *SLR* is a monthly magazine including product launches, marketplace analysis and ideas for retailers to improve their businesses.

Online Resources

InRetail
Website: www.inretail.co.uk

This is the leading recruitment website for the retail industry in the UK. It contains retail news, gives very useful descriptions of jobs within the industry, has a section exclusively for graduates and also a comprehensive list of jobs you can apply for by email.

InterQuest

Website: www.interquest.co.uk

If your area of interest in retail lies within IT then you should check out this website. The InterQuest Group Ltd provides IT personnel across the retail sector, including systems analysis, database administration and infrastructure support. It has a specialist candidate database for IT staff, either in permanent positions or interim staff for particular projects. More information is available from retail@interquest.co.uk

Retail Human Resources

Website: www.rhr.co.uk

This is the largest recruitment consultancy in the UK specialising in retail appointments. Retail Human Resources has 11 offices in the UK and handles vacancies in everything from buying, merchandising and distribution to human resources and technical & design.